In the Community

At the Hospital

By Julia Jaske

2 I see doctors at the hospital.

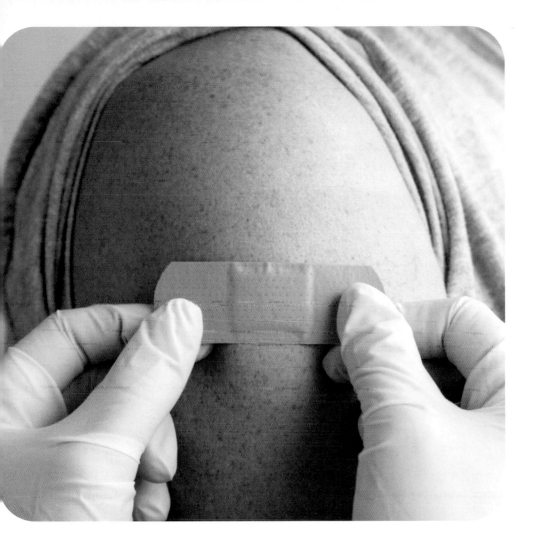

I see bandages at the hospital.

 4 I see stethoscopes at the hospital.

I see nurses at the hospital.

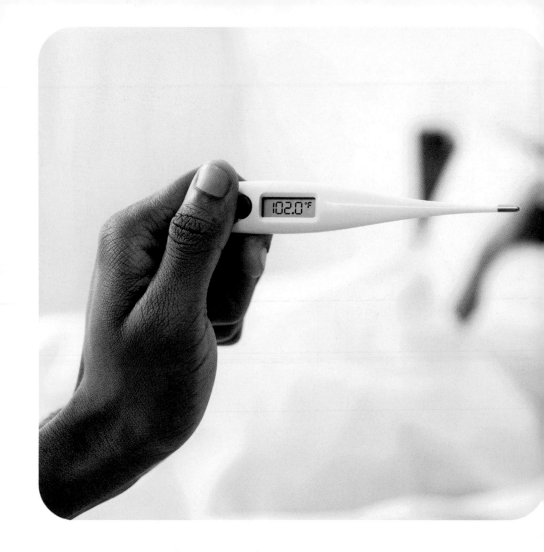

 I see thermometers
at the hospital.

I see medicine at the hospital.

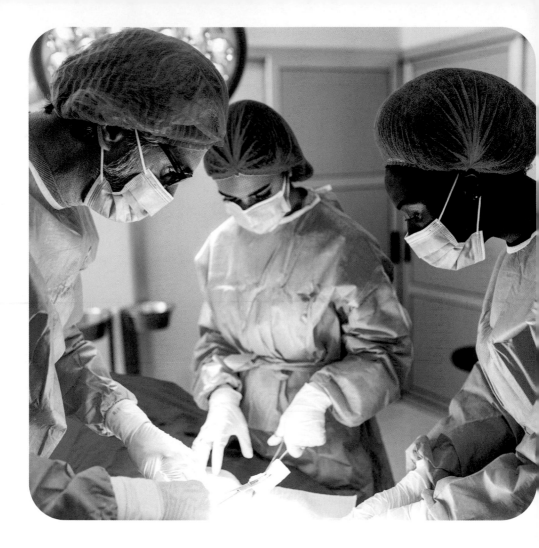

I see surgeons at the hospital.

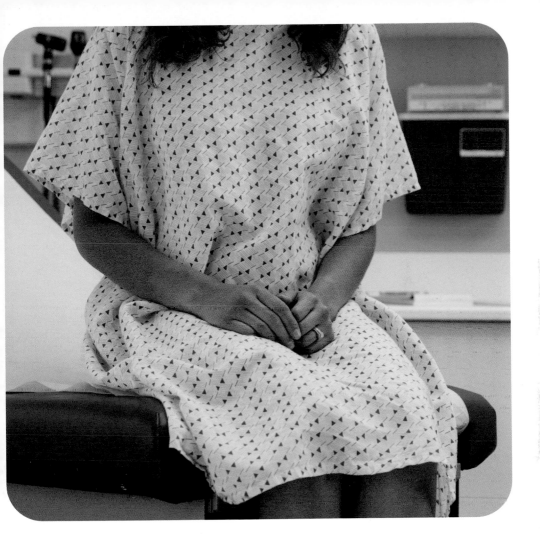

I see gowns at the hospital.

10 I see wheelchairs at the hospital.

I see patients at the hospital.

I see therapists at the hospital.

I see x-rays at the hospital.

hospital thermometers patients
doctors medicine therapists
bandages surgeons x-rays
stethoscopes gowns
nurses wheelchairs

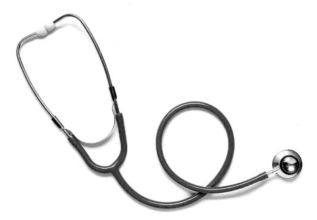

- I see doctors at the hospital.
- I see bandages at the hospital.
- I see stethoscopes at the hospital.
- I see nurses at the hospital.
- I see thermometers at the hospital.
- I see medicine at the hospital.
- I see surgeons at the hospital.
- I see gowns at the hospital.
- I see wheelchairs at the hospital.
- I see patients at the hospital.
- I see therapists at the hospital.
- I see x-rays at the hospital.

CHERRY BLOSSOM PRESS

Published in the United States of America by Cherry Lake Publishing Group
Ann Arbor, Michigan
www.cherrylakepublishing.com

Book Designer: Keri Riley

Photo Credits: cover: © LightField Studios/Shutterstock; page 1: © Drazen Zigic/Shutterstock; page 2: © Stokkete/Shutterstock; page 3: © FotoDuets/Shutterstock; page 4: © Stokkete/Shutterstock; page 5: © Monkey Business Images/Shutterstock; page 6: © Prostock-studio/Shutterstock; page 7: © Marian Weyo/Shutterstock; page 8: © Photoroyalty/Shutterstock; page 9: © Rocketclips, Inc./Shutterstock; page 10: © New Africa/Shutterstock; page 11: © PeopleImages.com – Yuri A/Shutterstock; page 12: © Ground Picture/Shutterstock; page 13: © Jelena Stanojkovic/Shutterstock; page 14: © Pixel-Shot/Shutterstock

Note from publisher: Websites change regularly, and their future contents are outside of our control. Supervise children when conducting any recommended online searches for extended learning opportunities.

Cherry Blossom Press is an imprint of Cherry Lake Publishing Group.

Library of Congress Cataloging-in-Publication Data

Names: Jaske, Julia, author.
Title: At the hospital / written by Julia Jaske.
Description: Ann Arbor, Michigan : Cherry Blossom Press, 2023. | Series: In the community | Audience: Grades K-1 | Summary: "At the Hospital explores the sights and sounds of the hospital. It covers people and objects found at the hospital. Uses the Whole Language approach to literacy, combining sight words and repetition to build recognition and confidence. Simple text makes reading these books easy and fun. Bold, colorful photographs that align directly with the text help readers with comprehension"– Provided by publisher.
Identifiers: LCCN 2023003180 | ISBN 9781668927199 (paperback) | ISBN 9781668929711 (ebook) | ISBN 9781668931196 (pdf)
Subjects: LCSH: Readers (Primary) | LCGFT: Readers (Publications).
Classification: LCC PE1119.2 .J363 2023 | DDC 428.6/2–dc23/eng/20230203
LC record available at https://lccn.loc.gov/2023003180

Printed in the United States of America
Corporate Graphics